New Testament

Scripture Mastery & Copywork

More by SherLynne Beach & Success Families

COPYWORK BOOKS:

- Cursive Jokes Copywork Volume 1: Write and Laugh
- Manuscript Jokes Copywork Volume1: Write and Laugh
- Proverbs for Children: Handwriting, Copy-Work and Memorization
- New Testament Scripture Mastery
- …more to come… (Old Testament, George Washington's Rules of Civility, Ben Franklin's Virtues, Virtues of Christ, etc.)

FAMILY JOKE BOOKS:

- A Pile of Giggles 1: Favorite Family Jokes
- A Pile of Giggles 2: Clean Acronyms, Puns, and One-Liners…For Teens and Their Families
- A Pile of Giggles 3: Clean Jokes…For Teens and Their Families
- …more to come…

MINDSET & FORGIVING WORKBOOKS:

- **Powerful Mind: A class workbook for adults and children**
- Baggage Be Gone: Clean It Out And Let It Go! Then Move Forward With Energy, Love, Peace and Joy
- …more to come…

OTHER BOOKS:

- Timeless Principles Of Raising Great Kids: by best-selling authors & mentors

COURSES (topics) coming to *www.SuccessFamilies.com*

- Mastering Mind Chatter
- Vision Board Training
- Goal Success to Glorify God
- …and more to come…

~NEW TESTAMENT~ SCRIPTURE MASTERY & COPYWORK

Manuscript and *Cursive Practice*

SherLynne Beach, Success Families

~New Testament~
Scripture Mastery & Copywork
Manuscript and Cursive Practice
© 2016 SherLynne Beach and Success Families, Mapleton
All rights reserved
ISBN-13: 978-1523840212
ISBN-10: 1523840218

Dedication

To God's Children Everywhere.

Contents

Books in the New Testament 3

Matthew 6:24 15

Matthew 11:28–30* 19

Matthew 16:15-19 24

Matthew 22:36–39* 34

Matthew 25:40 40

Matthew 28:19–20* 44

Luke 24:36-39 50

John 3:5 58

John 7:17 62

John 10:16 66

John 14:6* 70

John 14:15 74

John 17:3 77

Acts 2:36–38* 81

Acts 3:19–21* 89

Acts 7:55-56 96

Romans 1:16 101

1 Corinthians 6:19–20* 105

1 Corinthians 10:13 110

1 Corinthians 15:20-22 115

1 Corinthians 15:29 120

1 Corinthians 15:40-42 124

Galatians 5:22–23* 131

Ephesians 4:11-14 135

Philippians 4:13* 144

2 Thessalonians 2:1-3 147

2 Timothy 3:1-5 155

2 Timothy 3:15-17 (15*) 163

Hebrews 5:4 170

Hebrews 12:9* 174

James 1:5-6 178

James 2:17-18 183

1 Peter 4:6* 188

Revelation 14:6-7 192

Revelation 20:12-13 199

Scripture _____ 206

Scripture _____ 210

Scripture _____ 214

Scripture _____ 218

Scripture _____ 222

Scripture _____ 226

Scripture _____ 230

Scripture _____ 234

Scripture _____ 238

Scripture _____ 242

Introduction

This book is designed with any Christian family in mind. In my home we use it to help our children understand and learn key New Testament scriptures while practicing their handwriting (both manuscript and cursive).

This book is designed to be flexible. It has in it both manuscript and cursive practice pages as well as pages to explore the scripture's context, messages, and personal application.

We love studying scriptures together as a family and singing to learn them. In my home we study a verse over several days or weeks depending on the length of the passage. Do what works for your family.

Also, fun songs can be found to download for free (as of the date of printing this book) to help - master the verses in a very fun way. Here are the links:

Song for the Books in the New Testament:
- *https://www.lds.org/music/library/childrens-songbook/the-books-in-the-new-testament?lang=eng*

Scripture Mastery Songs:
- *http://lds.about.com/od/seminary/a/scripture_songs_5.htm* (available if there is a * by the scripture reference)

- *http://www.scripturemasterysongs.com/*

We hope you find this resource valuable, and invite you to check out SuccessFamilies and SherLynne Beach books and courses at *www.SuccessFamilies.com*

Additional Scripture Mastery Ideas

- Mark the passages
- Look up similar passages or verses to broaden the understanding of the principle or doctrine being taught
- Learn the Books
- Memorize the references and key words of each scripture mastery passage
- Scripture Chase—Use clues to help students practice quickly locating passages
- Story Chase—Give clues by making up scenarios that demonstrate the relevance of scripture mastery passages to everyday life.
- Test their memory of scripture mastery passages. Using clues like key words or scripture references, quotations from passages, or scenarios that illustrate the truths taught.
- Define words and phrases
- Identifying context (historical, cultural, and geographical), and the question or situation from which the content of the scripture passage arose.
- Identify more context—speaker, audience, purpose, other helpful insights.
- Describe how these truths are relevant to them.
- Write clues—create questions, scenarios, or other clues that illustrate the passages.
- Explain scripture passage - identify a word or phrase they think gives the meaning of the passage. Explain why that word or phrase is important
- Prepare a Devotional—summarize context, explain doctrines and principles, share meaningful experiences or examples, and testify of the doctrines and principles in the passages. using an object lesson
- Listening for scripture passages—Invite students to listen for scripture mastery passages in talks and lessons at church, and in discussions with family and friends.
- Present a message—Prepare 3- to 5-minute talks or family lessons based on scripture mastery passages.
- Share and testify of the experiences they have had with applying doctrines and principles.
- Set specific goals to live the principles found in scripture mastery passages. And report on the success in achieving that goal.
- One-Word Race—Challenge the children to say a scripture mastery passage one word per child at a time.

~New Testament~
Scripture Mastery

Manuscript and *Cursive Practice*

Books in the New Testament

> Matthew, Mark, Luke, John, the Acts and Romans,
> First and Second Corinthians,
> Galatians, Ephesians, Philippians, Colossians,
> First and Second Thessalonians,
> Timothy, Timothy, Titus, Philemon (fie-lee-mawn),
> Then to the Hebrews, Epistle of James,
> Peter, Peter, John, John, John, Jude, Revelation-
> These are the books of the New Testament.

Matthew, Mark, Luke,

John, the Acts and

Romans, First and Second

Corinthians, Galatians,

Ephesians, Philippians,

Colossians, First and

Second Thessalonians,

Timothy, Timothy, Titus,

Philemon (fie-lee-mawn),

Then to the Hebrews,

Epistle of James,

Peter, Peter, John,

John, John, Jude,

Revelation-

These are the books of

the New Testament.

Matthew, Mark, Luke, John,

the Acts and Romans,

First and Second Corinthians,

Galatians, Ephesians, Philippians,

Colossians, First and Second

Thessalonians, Timothy, Timothy,

Titus, Philemon (fie-lee-mawn),

Then to the Hebrews, Epistle

of James, Peter, Peter, John, John,

John, Jude, Revelation-

These are the books of

The New Testament.

Matthew 5:14–16

Key Phrase _____

---

14. Ye are the light of the world. A city that is set on an hill cannot be hid.

15. Neither do men light a candle, and put it under a bushel, but on a candlestick; and it giveth light unto all that are in the house.

16. Let your light so shine before men, that they may see your good works, and glorify your Father which is in heaven.

Define new words

_____

_____

_____

Who is speaking? _____

What is happening? _____

_____

What doctrine or principle is being taught?

_____

_____

_____

How can you apply this today?

_____

_____

_____

Draw the scene (context) of this verse or a picture of you applying this verse today.

14. Ye are the light of the world. A city that is set on an hill cannot be hid.

15. Neither do men light a candle, and put it under a bushel, but on a candlestick; and it

giveth light unto all that are in the house.

16. Let your light so shine before men, that they may see your good works, and glorify your Father which is in heaven.

14. Ye are the light of the world

A city that is set on an hill

cannot be hid.

15. Neither do men light a

candle, and put it under

a bushel, but on a candlestick;

and it giveth light unto all

that are in the house.

16. Let your light so shine before

men, that they may see your

good works, and glorify your

Father which is in heaven.

Matthew 6:24

Key Phrase _____

> 24. No man can serve two masters: for either he will hate the one, and love the other; or else he will hold to the one, and despise the other. Ye cannot serve God and mammon.

Define new words

_____

_____

_____

Who is speaking? _____

What is happening? _____

_____

What doctrine or principle is being taught?

_____
_____
_____

How can you apply this today?

_____
_____
_____

Draw the scene (context) of this verse or a picture of you applying this verse today.

24. No man can serve two masters: for either he will hate the one, and love the other; or else he will hold to the one, and despise the other. Ye cannot serve God and mammon.

24. No man can serve two masters: for either he will hate the one, and love the other; or else he will hold to the one, and despise the other. Ye cannot serve God and mammon.

Matthew 11:28-30*

Key Phrase _____

> 28. Come unto me, all ye that labour and are heavy laden, and I will give you rest.
>
> 29. Take my yoke upon you, and learn of me; for I am meek and lowly in heart: and ye shall find rest unto your souls.
>
> 30. For my yoke is easy, and my burden is light.

Define new words

_____

_____

_____

Who is speaking? _____

What is happening? _____

_____

What doctrine or principle is being taught? _____

_____

_____

_____

How can you apply this today?

_____

_____

_____

Draw the scene (context) of this verse or a picture of you applying this verse today.

28. Come unto me, all ye that labour and are heavy laden, and I will give you rest.

29. Take my yoke upon you, and learn of me; for I am meek and lowly in heart: and ye shall find rest unto your

souls.

30. For my yoke is easy,

and my burden is light.

28. Come unto me, all ye that

labour and are heavy laden, and

I will give you rest.

29. Take my yoke upon you,

and learn of me; for I am

meek and lowly in heart: and

ye shall find rest unto your

souls.

30. For my yoke is easy, and

my burden is light.

Matthew 16:15-19

Key Phrase _____

> 15. He saith unto them, But whom say ye that I am?
>
> 16. And Simon Peter answered and said, Thou art the Christ, the Son of the living God.
>
> 17. And Jesus answered and said unto him, Blessed art thou, Simon Barjona: for flesh and blood hath not revealed it unto thee, but my Father which is in heaven.
>
> 18. And I say also unto thee, That thou art Peter, and upon this rock I will build my church; and the gates of hell shall not prevail against it.
>
> 19. And I will give unto thee the keys of the kingdom of heaven: and whatsoever thou shalt bind on earth shall be bound in heaven: and whatsoever thou shalt loose on earth shall be loosed in heaven.

Define new words

_____

_____

_____

Who is speaking? _____

What is happening? _____

_____

What doctrine or principle is being taught? _____

_____

_____

_____

How can you apply this today?

_____

_____

_____

Draw the scene (context) of this verse or a picture of you applying this verse today.

15. He saith unto them,

But whom say ye that

I am?

16. And Simon Peter

answered and said, Thou

art the Christ, the Son

of the living God.

17. And Jesus answered

and said unto him,

Blessed art thou, Simon

Barjona: for flesh and

blood hath not revealed

it unto thee, but my

Father which is in

heaven.

18. And I say also unto

thee, That thou art

Peter, and upon this

rock I will build my

church; and the gates of

hell shall not prevail

against it.

19. And I will give unto

thee the keys of the

kingdom of heaven: and

whatsoever thou shalt

bind on earth shall be

bound in heaven: and

whatsoever thou shalt

loose on earth shall be

loosed in heaven.

15. He saith unto them, But

whom say ye that I am

16. And Simon Peter answered

and said, Thou art the Christ, the

Son of the living God.

17. And Jesus answered and said

unto him, Blessed art thou,

Simon Barjona: for flesh and

blood hath not revealed it unto

thee, but my Father which is in

heaven.

18. And I say also unto thee,

That thou art Peter, and upon

this rock I will build my

church; and the gates of hell

shall not prevail against it.

19. And I will give unto thee

the keys of the kingdom of

heaven: and whatsoever thou

shalt bind on earth shall be

bound in heaven: and whatsoever

thou shalt loose on earth shall be

loosed in heaven.

Matthew 22:36–39*

Key Phrase _____

---

36. Master, which is the great commandment in the law?

37. Jesus said unto him, Thou shalt love the Lord thy God with all thy heart, and with all thy soul, and with all thy mind.

38. This is the first and great commandment.

39. And the second is like unto it, Thou shalt love thy neighbour as thyself

---

Define new words

_____

_____

_____

Who is speaking? _____

What is happening? _____

_____

What doctrine or principle is being taught? _____

_____

_____

_____

How can you apply this today?

_____

_____

_____

Draw the scene (context) of this verse or a picture of you applying this verse today.

36. Master, which is the great commandment in the law?

37. Jesus said unto him, Thou shalt love the Lord thy God with all thy heart, and with all thy soul, and with all thy

Mind.

38. This is the first and great commandment.

39. And the second is like unto it, Thou shalt love thy neighbour as Thyself

36. Master, which is the great

commandment in the law?

37. Jesus said unto him, Thou

shalt love the Lord thy God

with all thy heart and with all

thy soul, and with all thy

mind.

38. This is the first and great

commandment.

39. And the second is like unto

it, Thou shalt love thy neighbor

as thyself.

Matthew 25:40

Key Phrase _____

> 40. And the King shall answer and say unto them, Verily I say unto you, Inasmuch as ye have done it unto one of the least of these my brethren, ye have done it unto me.

Define new words

_____
_____
_____

Who is speaking? _____

What is happening? _____

_____

What doctrine or principle is being taught? _____

_____

_____

_____

How can you apply this today?

_____

_____

_____

Draw the scene (context) of this verse or a picture of you applying this verse today.

40. And the King shall answer and say unto them, Verily I say unto you, In as much as ye have done it unto one of the least of these my brethren, ye have done it unto me.

40. And the King shall answer and say unto them, Verily I say unto you, Inasmuch as ye have done it unto one of the least of these my brethren, ye have done it unto me.

Matthew 28:19–20*

Key Phrase _____

> 19. Go ye therefore, and teach all nations, baptizing them in the name of the Father, and of the Son, and of the Holy Ghost:
>
> 20. Teaching them to observe all things whatsoever I have commanded you: and, lo, I am with you always, even unto the end of the world. Amen.

Define new words

_____

_____

_____

Who is speaking? _____

What is happening? _____

_____

What doctrine or principle is being taught? _____

_____

_____

_____

How can you apply this today?

_____

_____

_____

Draw the scene (context) of this verse or a picture of you applying this verse today.

19. Go ye therefore, and teach all nations, baptizing them in the name of the Father, and of the Son, and of the Holy Ghost:

20. Teaching them to observe all things

whatsoever I have commanded you: and, lo, I am with you always, even unto the end of the world. Amen.

19. Go ye therefore, and teach all

nations, baptizing them in the

name of the Father, and of the

Son, and of the Holy Ghost:

20. Teaching them to observe all

things whatsoever I have

commanded you: and, lo, I am

with you always, even unto the

end of the world. Amen.

Luke 24:36-39

Key Phrase _____

---

36. And as they thus spake, Jesus himself stood in the midst of them, and saith unto them, Peace be unto you.

37. But they were terrified and affrighted, and supposed that they had seen a spirit.

38. And he said unto them, Why are ye troubled? and why do thoughts arise in your hearts?

39. Behold my hands and my feet, that it is I myself: handle me, and see; for a spirit hath not flesh and bones, as ye see me have.

Define new words

_____

_____

_____

Who is speaking? _____

What is happening? _____

_____

What doctrine or principle is being taught? _____

_____

_____

_____

How can you apply this today?

_____

_____

_____

Draw the scene (context) of this verse or a picture of you applying this verse today.

36. And as they thus spake, Jesus himself stood in the midst of them, and saith unto them, Peace be unto you.

37. But they were terrified and affrighted, and supposed

that they had seen a

spirit.

38. And he said unto

them, Why are ye

troubled? and why do

thoughts arise in your

hearts?

39. Behold my hands and

my feet, that it is I myself: handle me, and see; for a spirit hath not flesh and bones, as ye see me have.

36. And as they thus spake, Jesus

himself stood in the midst of

them, and saith unto them, Peace

be unto you.

37. But they were terrified and

affrighted, and supposed that they

had seen a spirit.

38. And he said unto them, Why are ye troubled? and why do thoughts arise in your hearts?

39. Behold my hands and my feet, that it is I myself: handle

me, and see; for a spirit hath

not flesh and bones, as ye see

me have.

John 3:5

Key Phrase _____

> 5. Jesus answered, Verily, verily, I say unto thee, Except a man be born of water and of the Spirit, he cannot enter into the kingdom of God.

Define new words

_____

_____

_____

Who is speaking? _____

What is happening? _____

_____

What doctrine or principle is being taught? _____

_____

_____

_____

How can you apply this today?

_____

_____

_____

Draw the scene (context) of this verse or a picture of you applying this verse today.

5. Jesus answered, Verily, verily, I say unto thee, Except a man be born of water and of the Spirit, he cannot enter into the kingdom of God.

5. Jesus answered, Verily, verily, I say unto thee, Except a man be born of water and of the Spirit, he cannot enter into the kingdom of God.

John 7:17

Key Phrase _____

> 17. If any man will do his will, he shall know of the doctrine, whether it be of God, or whether I speak of myself.

Define new words

_____

_____

_____

Who is speaking? _____

What is happening? _____

_____

What doctrine or principle is being taught? _____

_____

_____

_____

How can you apply this today?

_____

_____

_____

Draw the scene (context) of this verse or a picture of you applying this verse today.

17. If any man will do his will, he shall know of the doctrine, whether it be of God, or whether I speak of myself.

17. If any man will do his

will, he shall know of the

doctrine, whether it be of God, or

whether I speak of myself.

John 10:16

Key Phrase _____

> 16. And other sheep I have, which are not of this fold: them also I must bring, and they shall hear my voice; and there shall be one fold, and one shepherd.

Define new words

_____

_____

_____

Who is speaking? _____

What is happening? _____

_____

What doctrine or principle is being taught? _____

_____

_____

_____

How can you apply this today?

_____

_____

_____

Draw the scene (context) of this verse or a picture of you applying this verse today.

16. And other sheep I have, which are not of this fold: them also I must bring, and they shall hear my voice; and there shall be one fold, and one shepherd.

16. And other sheep I have, which are not of this fold: them also I must bring, and they shall hear my voice; and there shall be one fold, and one shepherd.

John 14:6*

Key Phrase _____

> 6. Jesus saith unto him, I am the way, the truth, and the life: no man cometh unto the Father, but by me.

Define new words

_____

_____

_____

Who is speaking? _____

What is happening? _____

_____

What doctrine or principle is being taught? _____

_____

_____

_____

How can you apply this today?

_____

_____

_____

Draw the scene (context) of this verse or a picture of you applying this verse today.

6. Jesus saith unto him, I am the way, the truth, and the life: no man cometh unto the Father, but by me.

6. Jesus saith unto him, I am

the way, the truth, and the life:

no man cometh unto the

Father, but by me.

John 14:15

Key Phrase _____

> 15. If ye love me, keep my commandments.

Define new words

_____
_____
_____

Who is speaking? _____

What is happening? _____
_____

What doctrine or principle is being taught? _____

_____

_____

_____

How can you apply this today?

_____

_____

_____

Draw the scene (context) of this verse or a picture of you applying this verse today.

15. If ye love me, keep my commandments.

15. If ye love me, keep my commandments.

John 17:3

Key Phrase _____

> 3. And this is life eternal, that they might know thee the only true God, and Jesus Christ, whom thou hast sent.

Define new words

_____

_____

_____

Who is speaking? _____

What is happening? _____

_____

What doctrine or principle is being taught? _____

_____

_____

_____

How can you apply this today?

_____

_____

_____

Draw the scene (context) of this verse or a picture of you applying this verse today.

3. And this is life eternal, that they might know thee the only true God, and Jesus Christ, whom thou hast sent.

3. And this is life eternal, that

they might know thee the only

true God, and Jesus Christ, whom

thou hast sent.

Acts 2:36-38*

Key Phrase _____

> 36. Therefore let all the house of Israel know assuredly, that God hath made the same Jesus, whom ye have crucified, both Lord and Christ.
>
> 37. Now when they heard this, they were pricked in their heart, and said unto Peter and to the rest of the apostles, Men and brethren, what shall we do?
>
> 38. Then Peter said unto them, Repent, and be baptized every one of you in the name of Jesus Christ for the remission of sins, and ye shall receive the gift of the Holy Ghost.

Define new words

_____

_____

_____

Who is speaking? _____

What is happening? _____

_____

What doctrine or principle is being taught? _____

_____

_____

_____

How can you apply this today?

_____

_____

_____

Draw the scene (context) of this verse or a picture of you applying this verse today.

36. Therefore let all the house of Israel know assuredly, that God hath made the same Jesus, whom ye have crucified, both Lord and Christ.

37. Now when they heard this, they were pricked

in their heart, and said unto Peter and to the rest of the apostles, Men and brethren, what shall we do?

38. Then Peter said unto them, Repent, and be baptized every one of

you in the name of Jesus Christ for the remission of sins, and ye shall receive the gift of the Holy Ghost.

36. Therefore let all the house of

Israel know assuredly, that God

hath made the same Jesus, whom

ye have crucified, both Lord and

Christ.

37. Now when they heard this,

they were pricked in their heart,

and said unto Peter and to the

rest of the apostles, Men and

brethren, what shall we do?

38. Then Peter said unto them,

Repent, and be baptized every

one of you in the name of Jesus

Christ for the remission of sins,

and ye shall receive the gift of

the Holy Ghost.

Acts 3:19-21*

Key Phrase _____

---

19. Repent ye therefore, and be converted, that your sins may be blotted out, when the times of refreshing shall come from the presence of the Lord.

20. And he shall send Jesus Christ, which before was preached unto you:

21. Whom the heaven must receive until the times of restitution of all things, which God hath spoken by the mouth of all his holy prophets since the world began.

Define new words

_____

_____

_____

Who is speaking? _____

What is happening? _____

_____

What doctrine or principle is being taught? _____

_____

_____

_____

How can you apply this today?

_____

_____

_____

Draw the scene (context) of this verse or a picture of you applying this verse today.

19. Repent ye therefore, and be converted, that your sins may be blotted out, when the times of refreshing shall come from the presence of the Lord.

20. And he shall send

Jesus Christ, which before was preached unto you:

21. Whom the heaven must receive until the times of restitution of all things, which God hath spoken by the mouth of

all his holy prophets

since the world began.

19. Repent ye therefore, and be

converted, that your sins may

be blotted out, when the times of

refreshing shall come from the

presence of the Lord.

20. And he shall send Jesus Christ, which before was preached unto you:

21. Whom the heaven must receive until the times of

restitution of all things, which

God hath spoken by the mouth

of all his holy prophets since the

world began.

Acts 7:55-56

Key Phrase _____

> 55. But he, being full of the Holy Ghost, looked up stedfastly into heaven, and saw the glory of God, and Jesus standing on the right hand of God,
>
> 56. And said, Behold, I see the heavens opened, and the Son of man standing on the right hand of God.

Define new words

_____

_____

_____

Who is speaking? _____

What is happening? _____

_____

What doctrine or principle is being taught? _____

_____

_____

_____

How can you apply this today?

_____

_____

_____

Draw the scene (context) of this verse or a picture of you applying this verse today.

55. But he, being full of the Holy Ghost, Looked up stedfastly into heaven, and saw the glory of God, and Jesus standing on the right hand of God,

56. And said, Behold, I

see the heavens opened,

and the Son of man

standing on the right

hand of God.

55. But he, being full of the

Holy Ghost, looked up stedfastly

into heaven, and saw the glory

of God, and Jesus standing on

the right hand of God,

56. And said, Behold, I see the

heavens opened, and the Son of

man standing on the right

hand of God.

Romans 1:16

Key Phrase _____

> 16. For I am not ashamed of the gospel of Christ: for it is the power of God unto salvation to every one that believeth; to the Jew first, and also to the Greek.

Define new words

_____

_____

_____

Who is speaking? _____

What is happening? _____

_____

What doctrine or principle is being taught? _____

_____

_____

_____

How can you apply this today?

_____

_____

_____

Draw the scene (context) of this verse or a picture of you applying this verse today.

16. For I am not ashamed of the gospel of Christ: for it is the power of God unto salvation to every one that believeth; to the Jew first, and also to the Greek.

16. For I am not ashamed of

the gospel of Christ: for it is the

power of God unto salvation to

every one that believeth; to the

Jew first, and also to the Greek.

1 Corinthians 6:19–20*

Key Phrase _____

---

19. What? know ye not that your body is the temple of the Holy Ghost which is in you, which ye have of God, and ye are not your own?

20. For ye are bought with a price: therefore glorify God in your body, and in your spirit, which are God's.

Define new words

_____

_____

_____

Who is speaking? _____

What is happening? _____

_____

What doctrine or principle is being taught? _____

_____

_____

_____

How can you apply this today?

_____

_____

_____

Draw the scene (context) of this verse or a picture of you applying this verse today.

19. What? know ye not that your body is the temple of the Holy Ghost which is in you, which ye have of God, and ye are not your own?

20. For ye are bought with a price: therefore

glorify God in your

body, and in your

spirit, which are God's.

19. What? know ye not that

your body is the temple of the

Holy Ghost which is in you,

which ye have of God, and ye

are not your own?

20. For ye are bought with a

price: therefore glorify God in

your body, and in your spirit,

which are God's.

1 Corinthians 10:13

Key Phrase _____

> 13. There hath no temptation taken you but such as is common to man: but God is faithful, who will not suffer you to be tempted above that ye are able; but will with the temptation also make a way to escape, that ye may be able to bear it.

Define new words

_____

_____

_____

Who is speaking? _____

What is happening? _____

_____

What doctrine or principle is being taught? _____

_____

_____

_____

How can you apply this today?

_____

_____

_____

Draw the scene (context) of this verse or a picture of you applying this verse today.

13. There hath no temptation taken you but such as is common to man: but God is faithful, who will not suffer you to be tempted above that ye are able; but will with the

temptation also make a

way to escape, that ye

may be able to bear it.

13. There hath no temptation

taken you but such as is

common to man: but God is

faithful, who will not suffer you

to be tempted above that ye are

able; but will with the

temptation also make a way to

escape, that ye may be able to

bear it.

1 Corinthians 15:20-22

Key Phrase _____

> 20. But now is Christ risen from the dead, and become the first fruits of them that slept.
>
> 21. For since by man came death, by man came also the resurrection of the dead.
>
> 22. For as in Adam all die, even so in Christ shall all be made alive.

Define new words

_____

_____

_____

Who is speaking? _____

What is happening? _____

_____

What doctrine or principle is being taught? _____

_____

_____

_____

How can you apply this today?

_____

_____

_____

Draw the scene (context) of this verse or a picture of you applying this verse today.

20. But now is Christ risen from the dead, and become the first fruits of them that slept.

21. For since by man came death, by man came also the resurrection of the dead.

22. For as in Adam all die, even so in Christ shall all be made alive.

20. But now is Christ risen from the dead, and become the first fruits of them that slept.

21. For since by man came death, by man came also the resurrection of the dead.

22. For as in Adam all die, even so in Christ shall all be made alive.

1 Corinthians 15:29

Key Phrase _____

> 29. Else what shall they do which are baptized for the dead, if the dead rise not at all? why are they then baptized for the dead?

Define new words

_____

_____

_____

Who is speaking? _____

What is happening? _____

_____

What doctrine or principle is being taught? _____

_____

_____

_____

How can you apply this today?

_____

_____

_____

Draw the scene (context) of this verse or a picture of you applying this verse today.

29. Else what shall they do which are baptized for the dead, if the dead rise not at all? why are they then baptized for the dead?

29. Else what shall they do

which are baptized for the dead,

if the dead rise not at all?

Why are they then baptized for

the dead?

1 Corinthians 15:40-42

Key Phrase _____

> 40. There are also celestial bodies, and bodies terrestrial: but the glory of the celestial is one, and the glory of the terrestrial is another.
>
> 41. There is one glory of the sun, and another glory of the moon, and another glory of the stars: for one star differeth from another star in glory.
>
> 42. So also is the resurrection of the dead. It is sown in corruption; it is raised in incorruption:

Define new words

_____

_____

_____

Who is speaking? _____

What is happening? _____

_____

124

What doctrine or principle is being taught? _____

_____

_____

_____

How can you apply this today?

_____

_____

_____

Draw the scene (context) of this verse or a picture of you applying this verse today.

40. There are also celestial bodies, and bodies terrestrial: but the glory of the celestial is one, and the glory of the terrestrial is another.

41. There is one glory

of the sun, and another glory of the moon, and another glory of the stars: for one star differeth from another star in glory.

42. So also is the resurrection of the

dead. It is sown in

corruption; it is raised

in incorruption:

40. There are also celestial bodies, and bodies terrestrial: but the glory of the celestial is one, and

the glory of the terrestrial is

another.

41. There is one glory of the

sun, and another glory of the

moon, and another glory of the

stars: for one star differeth from

another star in glory.

42. So also is the resurrection of

the dead. It is sown in

corruption; it is raised in

incorruption:

Galatians 5:22-23*

Key Phrase _____

> 22. But the fruit of the Spirit is love, joy, peace, longsuffering, gentleness, goodness, faith,
>
> 23. Meekness, temperance: against such there is no law.

Define new words

_____

_____

_____

Who is speaking? _____

What is happening? _____

_____

What doctrine or principle is being taught? _____

_____

_____

_____

How can you apply this today?

_____

_____

_____

Draw the scene (context) of this verse or a picture of you applying this verse today.

22. But the fruit of the Spirit is love, joy, peace, longsuffering, gentleness, goodness, faith,

23. Meekness, temperance: against such there is no law.

22. But the fruit of the Spirit is

love, joy, peace, longsuffering,

gentleness, goodness, faith,

23. Meekness, temperance: against

such there is no law.

Ephesians 4:11-14

Key Phrase _____

---

11. And he gave some, apostles; and some, prophets; and some, evangelists; and some, pastors and teachers;

12. For the perfecting of the saints, for the work of the ministry, for the edifying of the body of Christ:

13. Till we all come in the unity of the faith, and of the knowledge of the Son of God, unto a perfect man, unto the measure of the stature of the fulness of Christ:

14. That we henceforth be no more children, tossed to and fro, and carried about with every wind of doctrine, by the sleight of men, and cunning craftiness, whereby they lie in wait to deceive;

Define new words

_____

_____

_____

Who is speaking? _____

What is happening? _____

_____

What doctrine or principle is being taught? _____

_____

_____

_____

How can you apply this today?

_____

_____

_____

Draw the scene (context) of this verse or a picture of you applying this verse today.

11. And he gave some,

apostles; and some,

prophets; and some,

evangelists; and some,

pastors and teachers;

12. For the perfecting

of the saints, for the

Work of the ministry,

for the edifying of the

body of Christ:

13. Till we all come in

the unity of the faith,

and of the knowledge of

the Son of God, unto a

perfect man, unto the

measure of the stature

of the fulness of

Christ:

14. That we henceforth

be no more children,

tossed to and fro, and

carried about with every

wind of doctrine, by

the sleight of men,

and cunning craftiness,

whereby they lie in wait

to deceive;

11. And he gave some, apostles;

and some, prophets; and some,

evangelists; and some, pastors

and teachers;

12. For the perfecting of the

saints, for the work of the

ministry, for the edifying of the

body of Christ:

13. Till we all come in the

unity of the faith, and of the

knowledge of the Son of God,

unto a perfect man, unto the

measure of the stature of the

fulness of Christ:

14. That we henceforth be no

more children, tossed to and fro,

and carried about with every

wind of doctrine, by the sleight

of men, and cunning craftiness,

whereby they lie in wait to

deceive;

Philippians 4:13*

Key Phrase _____

> 13. I can do all things through Christ which strengtheneth me.

Define new words

_____

_____

_____

Who is speaking? _____

What is happening? _____

_____

What doctrine or principle is being taught? _____

How can you apply this today?

Draw the scene (context) of this verse or a picture of you applying this verse today.

13. I can do all things through Christ which strengtheneth me.

13. I can do all things through Christ which strengtheneth me.

2 Thessalonians 2:1-3

Key Phrase _____

> 1. Now we beseech you, brethren, by the coming of our Lord Jesus Christ, and by our gathering together unto him,
>
> 2. That ye be not soon shaken in mind, or be troubled, neither by spirit, nor by word, nor by letter as from us, as that the day of Christ is at hand.
>
> 3. Let no man deceive you by any means: for that day shall not come, except there come a falling away first, and that man of sin be revealed, the son of perdition;

Define new words

_____

_____

_____

Who is speaking? _____

What is happening? _____

_____

What doctrine or principle is being taught? _____
_____
_____
_____

How can you apply this today?
_____
_____
_____

Draw the scene (context) of this verse or a picture of you applying this verse today.

1. Now we beseech you, brethren, by the coming of our Lord Jesus Christ, and by our gathering together unto him,

2. That ye be not soon shaken in mind, or be

troubled, neither by spirit, nor by word, nor by letter as from us, as that the day of Christ is at hand.

3. Let no man deceive you by any means: for that day shall not come,

except there come a

falling away first, and

that man of sin be

revealed, the son of

perdition;

1. Now we beseech you, brethren,

by the coming of our Lord Jesus

Christ, and by our gathering

together unto him,

2. That ye be not soon shaken

in mind, or be troubled, neither

by spirit, nor by word, nor by

letter as from us, as that the

day of Christ is at hand.

3. Let no man deceive you by

any means: for that day shall

not come, except there come a

falling away first, and that

man of sin be revealed, the son

of perdition;

2 Timothy 3:1-5

Key Phrase _____

> 1. This know also, that in the last days perilous times shall come.
>
> 2. For men shall be lovers of their own selves, covetous, boasters, proud, blasphemers, disobedient to parents, unthankful, unholy,
>
> 3. Without natural affection, trucebreakers, false accusers, incontinent, fierce, despisers of those that are good,
>
> 4. Traitors, heady, highminded, lovers of pleasures more than lovers of God;
>
> 5. Having a form of godliness, but denying the power thereof: from such turn away.

Define new words

_____

_____

_____

Who is speaking? _____

What is happening? _____

_____

What doctrine or principle is being taught? _____

How can you apply this today?

Draw the scene (context) of this verse or a picture of you applying this verse today.

1. This know also, that in the last days perilous times shall come.

2. For men shall be lovers of their own selves, covetous, boasters, proud,

blasphemers, disobedient

to parents, unthankful,

unholy,

3. Without natural

affection,

trucebreakers, false

accusers, incontinent,

fierce, despisers of

those that are good,

4. Traitors, heady, highminded, lovers of pleasures more than lovers of God;

5. Having a form of godliness, but denying the power thereof: from

such turn away.

1. This know also, that in the last days perilous times shall come.
2. For men shall be lovers of their own selves, covetous, boasters, proud, blasphemers,

disobedient to parents,

unthankful, unholy,

3. Without natural affection,

trucebreakers, false accusers,

incontinent, fierce, despisers of

those that are good,

4. Traitors, heady, highminded,

lovers of pleasures more than

lovers of God;

5. Having a form of godliness,

but denying the power thereof:

from such turn away.

2 Timothy 3:15-17 (15*)

Key Phrase _____

---

15. And that from a child thou hast known the holy scriptures, which are able to make thee wise unto salvation through faith which is in Christ Jesus.

16. All scripture is given by inspiration of God, and is profitable for doctrine, for reproof, for correction, for instruction in righteousness:

17. That the man of God may be perfect, thoroughly furnished unto all good works.

Define new words

_____

_____

_____

Who is speaking? _____

What is happening? _____

_____

What doctrine or principle is being taught? _____

_____

_____

_____

How can you apply this today?

_____

_____

_____

Draw the scene (context) of this verse or a picture of you applying this verse today.

15. And that from a child thou hast known the holy scriptures, which are able to make thee wise unto salvation through faith which is in Christ Jesus.

16. All scripture is given by inspiration of God, and is profitable for doctrine, for reproof, for correction, for instruction in righteousness:

17. That the man of God

may be perfect,

thoroughly furnished

unto all good works.

15. And that from a child thou

hast known the holy scriptures,

which are able to make thee wise

unto salvation through faith

which is in Christ Jesus.

16. All scripture is given by

inspiration of God, and is

profitable for doctrine, for reproof,

for correction, for instruction in

righteousness:

17. That the man of God may be perfect, thoroughly furnished unto all good works.

Hebrews 5:4

Key Phrase _____

> 4. And no man taketh this honour unto himself, but he that is called of God, as was Aaron.

Define new words

_____

_____

_____

Who is speaking? _____

What is happening? _____

_____

What doctrine or principle is being taught? _____

_____

_____

_____

How can you apply this today?

_____

_____

_____

Draw the scene (context) of this verse or a picture of you applying this verse today.

4. And no man taketh this honour unto himself, but he that is called of God, as was Aaron.

4. And no man taketh this honour unto himself, but he that is called of God, as was Aaron.

Hebrews 12:9*

Key Phrase _____

> 9. Furthermore we have had fathers of our flesh which corrected us, and we gave them reverence: shall we not much rather be in subjection unto the Father of spirits, and live?

Define new words

_____

_____

_____

Who is speaking? _____

What is happening? _____

_____

What doctrine or principle is being taught?

How can you apply this today?

Draw the scene (context) of this verse or a picture of you applying this verse today.

9. Furthermore we have had fathers of our flesh which corrected us, and we gave them reverence: shall we not much rather be in subjection unto the Father of spirits, and live?

9. Furthermore we have had fathers of our flesh which corrected us, and we gave them reverence: shall we not much rather be in subjection unto the Father of spirits, and live?

James 1:5-6

Key Phrase _____

---

5. If any of you lack wisdom, let him ask of God, that giveth to all men liberally, and upbraideth not; and it shall be given him.

6. But let him ask in faith, nothing wavering. For he that wavereth is like a wave of the sea driven with the wind and tossed.

Define new words

_____

_____

_____

Who is speaking? _____

What is happening? _____

_____

What doctrine or principle is being taught? _____

_____

_____

_____

How can you apply this today?

_____

_____

_____

Draw the scene (context) of this verse or a picture of you applying this verse today.

5. If any of you lack wisdom, let him ask of God, that giveth to all men liberally, and upbraideth not; and it shall be given him.

6. But let him ask in faith, nothing wavering.

For he that wavereth is

like a wave of the sea

driven with the wind and

tossed.

5. If any of you lack wisdom,

let him ask of God, that giveth

to all men liberally, and

upbraideth not; and it shall be

given him.

6. But let him ask in faith,

nothing wavering. For he that

wavereth is like a wave of the sea

driven with the wind and tossed.

James 2:17-18

Key Phrase _____

---

17. Even so faith, if it hath not works, is dead, being alone.

18. Yea, a man may say, Thou hast faith, and I have works: shew me thy faith without thy works, and I will shew thee my faith by my works.

Define new words

_____

_____

_____

Who is speaking? _____

What is happening? _____

_____

What doctrine or principle is being taught? _____

_____

_____

_____

How can you apply this today?

_____

_____

_____

Draw the scene (context) of this verse or a picture of you applying this verse today.

17. Even so faith, if it hath not works, is dead, being alone.

18. Yea, a man may say, Thou hast faith, and I have works: shew me thy faith without thy works, and I will shew thee my

faith by my works.

17. Even so faith, if it hath not

works, is dead, being alone.

18. Yea, a man may say, Thou

hast faith, and I have works:

shew me thy faith without thy

works, and I will shew thee my

faith by my works.

1 Peter 4:6*

Key Phrase _____

> 6. For for this cause was the gospel preached also to them that are dead, that they might be judged according to men in the flesh, but live according to God in the spirit.

Define new words

_____

_____

_____

Who is speaking? _____

What is happening? _____

_____

What doctrine or principle is being taught? _____

_____

_____

_____

How can you apply this today?

_____

_____

_____

Draw the scene (context) of this verse or a picture of you applying this verse today.

6. For for this cause was the gospel preached also to them that are dead, that they might be judged according to men in the flesh, but live according to God in the spirit.

6. For for this cause was the

gospel preached also to them that

are dead, that they might be

judged according to men in the

flesh, but live according to God

in the spirit.

Revelation 14:6-7

Key Phrase _____

---

6. And I saw another angel fly in the midst of heaven, having the everlasting gospel to preach unto them that dwell on the earth, and to every nation, and kindred, and tongue, and people,

7. Saying with a loud voice, Fear God, and give glory to him; for the hour of his judgment is come: and worship him that made heaven, and earth, and the sea, and the fountains of waters.

Define new words

_____

_____

_____

Who is speaking? _____

What is happening? _____

_____

What doctrine or principle is being taught? _____

_____

_____

_____

How can you apply this today?

_____

_____

_____

Draw the scene (context) of this verse or a picture of you applying this verse today.

6. And I saw another angel fly in the midst of heaven, having the everlasting gospel to preach unto them that dwell on the earth, and to every nation, and kindred, and tongue, and

people,

7. Saying with a loud voice, Fear God, and give glory to him; for the hour of his judgment is come: and worship him that made heaven, and earth, and the sea, and

the fountains of waters.

6. And I saw another angel fly in the midst of heaven, having the everlasting gospel to preach unto them that dwell on the earth, and to every nation, and

kindred, and tongue, and people,

7. Saying with a loud voice,

Fear God, and give glory to

him; for the hour of his

judgment is come: and worship

him that made heaven, and

earth, and the sea, and the

fountains of waters.

Revelation 20:12-13

Key Phrase _____

> 12. And I saw the dead, small and great, stand before God; and the books were opened: and another book was opened, which is the book of life: and the dead were judged out of those things which were written in the books, according to their works.
>
> 13. And the sea gave up the dead which were in it; and death and hell delivered up the dead which were in them: and they were judged every man according to their works.

Define new words

_____

_____

_____

Who is speaking? _____

What is happening? _____

_____

What doctrine or principle is being taught? _____

_____

_____

How can you apply this today?

_____

_____

_____

Draw the scene (context) of this verse or a picture of you applying this verse today.

12. And I saw the dead, small and great, stand before God; and the books were opened: and another book was opened, which is the book of life: and the dead were judged out of those

things which were written in the books, according to their works.

13. And the sea gave up the dead which were in it; and death and hell delivered up the dead

which were in them: and

they were judged every

man according to their

works.

12. And I saw the dead, small

and great, stand before God; and

the books were opened: and

another book was opened, which

is the book of life: and the dead

were judged out of those things

which were written in the books,

according to their works.

13. And the sea gave up the dead

which were in it; and death

and hell delivered up the dead

which were in them: and they

were judged every man according

to their works.

Scripture _____

Key Phrase _____

Define new words

_____

_____

_____

Who is speaking? _____

What is happening? _____

_____

What doctrine or principle is being taught? _____

_____

_____

_____

How can you apply this today?

_____

_____

_____

Draw the scene (context) of this verse or a picture of you applying this verse today.

Scripture _____

Key Phrase _____

Define new words

_____

_____

_____

Who is speaking? _____

What is happening? _____

_____

What doctrine or principle is being taught? _____

_____

_____

_____

How can you apply this today?

_____

_____

_____

Draw the scene (context) of this verse or a picture of you applying this verse today.

Scripture _____

Key Phrase _____

Define new words

_____

_____

_____

Who is speaking? _____

What is happening? _____

_____

What doctrine or principle is being taught? _____

_____

_____

_____

How can you apply this today?

_____

_____

_____

Draw the scene (context) of this verse or a picture of you applying this verse today.

Scripture _____

Key Phrase _____

[ ]

Define new words

_____

_____

_____

Who is speaking? _____

What is happening? _____

_____

What doctrine or principle is being taught? _____

_____

_____

_____

How can you apply this today?

_____

_____

_____

Draw the scene (context) of this verse or a picture of you applying this verse today.

Scripture _____
Key Phrase _____

```
┌─────────────────────────────────────────────────────┐
│                                                     │
│                                                     │
│                                                     │
│                                                     │
│                                                     │
│                                                     │
└─────────────────────────────────────────────────────┘
```

Define new words

_____

_____

_____

Who is speaking? _____

What is happening? _____

_____

What doctrine or principle is being taught? _____

_____

_____

_____

How can you apply this today?

_____

_____

_____

Draw the scene (context) of this verse or a picture of you applying this verse today.

Scripture _____

Key Phrase _____

```
┌─────────────────────────────────────────────┐
│                                             │
│                                             │
│                                             │
│                                             │
│                                             │
│                                             │
└─────────────────────────────────────────────┘
```

Define new words

_____

_____

_____

Who is speaking? _____

What is happening? _____

_____

What doctrine or principle is being taught? _____

_____

_____

_____

How can you apply this today?

_____

_____

_____

Draw the scene (context) of this verse or a picture of you applying this verse today.

Scripture _____

Key Phrase _____

Define new words

_____

_____

_____

Who is speaking? _____

What is happening? _____

_____

What doctrine or principle is being taught? _____

_____

_____

_____

How can you apply this today?

_____

_____

_____

Draw the scene (context) of this verse or a picture of you applying this verse today.

Scripture _____

Key Phrase _____

[ ]

Define new words

_____
_____
_____

Who is speaking?_____

What is happening? _____

_____

What doctrine or principle is being taught? _____

_____

_____

_____

How can you apply this today?

_____

_____

_____

Draw the scene (context) of this verse or a picture of you applying this verse today.

Scripture _____

Key Phrase _____

```
┌─────────────────────────────────────────────────────────┐
│                                                         │
│                                                         │
│                                                         │
│                                                         │
│                                                         │
│                                                         │
└─────────────────────────────────────────────────────────┘
```

Define new words

_____

_____

_____

Who is speaking? _____

What is happening? _____

_____

What doctrine or principle is being taught? _____

_____

_____

_____

How can you apply this today?

_____

_____

_____

Draw the scene (context) of this verse or a picture of you applying this verse today.

Scripture _____

Key Phrase _____

[ ]

Define new words

_____

_____

_____

Who is speaking? _____

What is happening? _____

_____

What doctrine or principle is being taught? _____

_____

_____

_____

How can you apply this today?

_____

_____

_____

Draw the scene (context) of this verse or a picture of you applying this verse today.

Sources

Song for the Books in the New Testament:
- *https://www.lds.org/music/library/childrens-songbook/the-books-in-the-new-testament?lang=eng*

Scripture Mastery Songs:
- *http://lds.about.com/od/seminary/a/scripture_songs_5.htm* (available if there is a * by the scripture reference)

- *http://www.scripturemasterysongs.com/*

List of Scriptures
- https://www.lds.org/manual/book-of-mormon-seminary-teacher-manual-2013/appendix/lesson-166?lang=eng
- http://utahvalley360.com/2013/08/21/new-scripture-mastery-passages-announced-for-lds-seminaries/

Scripture Mastery Ideas
- http://seminary.lds.org/mastery/scripture-mastery/methods-for-teaching?lang=eng
- http://nwseminaryshare.weebly.com/scripture-mastery-activities.html

Made in the USA
Middletown, DE
18 June 2024